W9-ATG-906

JESSE OWENS
LEGENDARY TRACK STAR

Famous African Americans

Patricia and Fredrick McKissack

Enslow Elementary
an imprint of
Enslow Publishers, Inc.

40 Industrial Road
Box 398
Berkeley Heights, NJ 07922
USA

http://www.enslow.com

To Our Friend, (Sir) Christopher Powell

Enslow Elementary, an imprint of Enslow Publishers, Inc.

Enslow Elementary® is a registered trademark of Enslow Publishers, Inc.

Copyright © 2013 by Enslow Publishers, Inc.

Revised edition of *Jesse Owens: Olympic Star* © 1992

Library of Congress Cataloging-in-Publication Data
    McKissack, Pat, 1944-
      Jesse Owens : legendary track star / Patricia and Fredrick McKissack.
        p. cm. — (Famous African Americans)
      Includes index.
      Summary: "A simple biography about Jesse Owens for early readers"—
    Provided by publisher.
      ISBN 978-0-7660-4104-2
      1. Owens, Jesse, 1913-1980—Juvenile literature. 2. Track and field ath-
    letes—United States—Biography—Juvenile literature. 3. African
    American track and field athletes—Biography—Juvenile literature. I.
    McKissack, Fredrick. II. Title.
      GV697.O9M34 2013
      796.42092—dc23
                                    2012009935

Future editions

Paperback ISBN: 978-1-4644-0199-2

ePUB ISBN: 978-1-4645-1112-7

PDF ISBN: 978-1-4646-1112-4

Printed in the United States of America

082012 Lake Book Manufacturing, Inc., Melrose Park, IL

10 9 8 7 6 5 4 3 2 1

To Our Readers: We have done our best to make sure all Internet Addresses in this book were active and appropriate when we went to press. However, the author and the publisher have no control over and assume no liability for the material available on those Internet sites or on other Web sites they may link to. Any comments or suggestions can be sent by e-mail to comments@enslow.com or to the address on the back cover.

Every effort has been made to locate all copyright holders of material used in this book. If any errors or omissions have occurred, corrections will be made in future editions of this book.

♻ Enslow Publishers, Inc., is committed to printing our books on recycled paper. The paper in every book contains 10% to 30% post-consumer waste (PCW). The cover board on the outside of each book contains 100% PCW. Our goal is to do our part to help young people and the environment too!

Illustration Credits: Michael David Biegel, pp. 7, 8, 10, 13; The Ohio State University Archives, pp. 1, 3, 4, 14, 16, 20.

Cover Credit: The Ohio State University Archives

Words in bold type are are explained in Words to Know on page 22.

Series Consultant:
Russell Adams, PhD
Emeritus Professor
Afro-American Studies
Howard University

CONTENTS

Jesse Owens was one of the world's greatest track and field stars.

CHAPTER 1
FROM J.C. TO JESSE

Henry Owens was a poor farmer in Oakville, Alabama. His wife, Emma, washed and ironed other people's clothes for extra money. The Owens family worked very hard. But they were still poor.

Henry Owens and his family were sharecroppers. A big landowner let them grow cotton on a small piece of his land. They gave most of their cotton to the landowner to pay for the land. They sold the little bit that was left so they could buy food and other things they needed. They could not save any money.

James Cleveland Owens was born in 1913. He was Henry and Emma's tenth child. They called him J.C. He was a sickly baby. His parents were afraid that he might not live.

J.C. was sick every winter. His lungs were weak. J.C.'s mother and father did not have money to pay a doctor. They took care of him the best way they could.

J.C.'s brothers and sisters helped their parents with the farm. They didn't have much time for school. They spent long hot days in the sun picking cotton. Some chopped the cotton, and some took the seeds out of the fuzzy blossoms.

J.C.'s father wanted a better life for his family. In 1922 he sold his mule. The family used the money to move to Cleveland, Ohio.

Henry Owens could not find steady work in Cleveland. But J.C. could go to school. On his first day at his new school, the teacher asked J.C. what his name was. She heard him say "Jesse," not J.C. From then on, everyone called him Jesse.

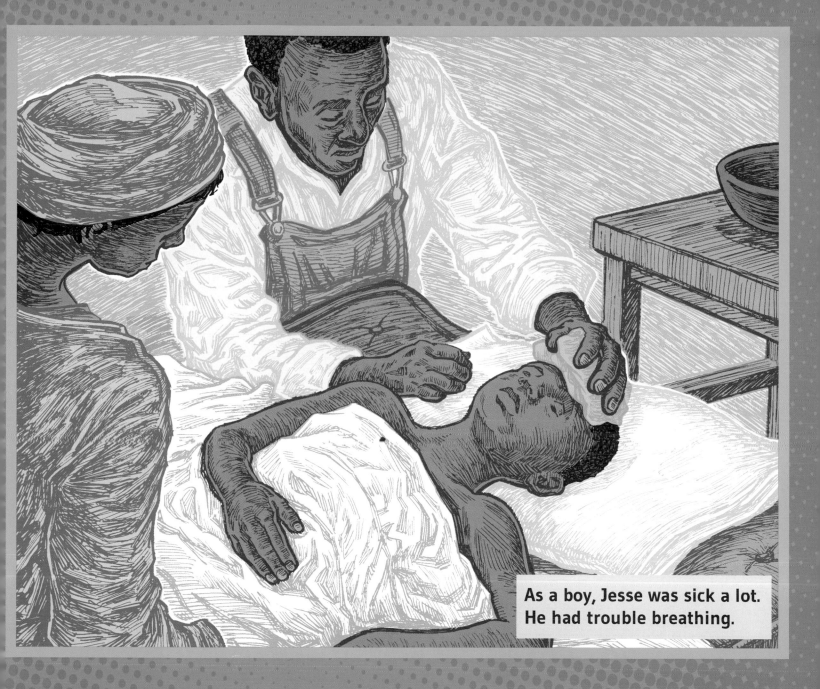

As a boy, Jesse was sick a lot. He had trouble breathing.

Running track helped Jesse become healthy. He worked with Coach Riley to become a better runner.

CHAPTER 2
THE BUCKEYE BULLET

When Jesse was fourteen years old, the coach of the junior high school track team asked him to be on the team. The coach's name was Charles Riley. Every day Jesse got up early and met Coach Riley at the track.

Jesse's lungs were still bad, and he was often sick. He trained with Coach Riley every morning. Running helped Jesse's lungs, and he grew stronger. And he was even running faster.

By the time he was in high school, Jesse was making a name for himself. Everybody at Cleveland East Technical High School was proud of his track records. He worked very hard to become a fast runner and a good jumper.

He ran **dashes**, and did **high jumps** and **broad jumps** (long jumps). And he broke national high school records almost every time he ran or jumped. Jesse was asked to

Jesse's hard work paid off. He could run faster and jump farther than anyone else.

attend Ohio State University and run for the track team. But he told track coach Larry Snyder that he could not go. Jesse had to work to help his family because his father still wasn't working.

Coach Snyder wanted Jesse to run on the Ohio State team. The coach helped Henry Owens get a job as a janitor at the university. Now Jesse did not have to work to help his family. He could work to pay his own way through school.

Jesse trained harder and harder. He wanted to be the best. His hard work paid off. On May 25, 1935, Jesse broke three **world records** and tied another record at the University of Michigan at Ann Arbor.

The Ohio State sports teams were nicknamed the Buckeyes. So after that day, people started calling Jesse "the Buckeye Bullet." He was on his way to the 1936 **Olympics** in Berlin, Germany.

CHAPTER 3
THE BERLIN OLYMPICS

. . . .

There were 66 Americans on the 1936 Summer Olympic **track and field** team. Ten of them were African Americans.

Adolf Hitler, the leader of Germany, came to the games on the opening day. The large crowd cheered for him. They raised their arms and shouted "**Heil Hitler!**"

Hitler was a **Nazi**. He believed that Germans were the "master race." He said they would rule the world one day. He also said that Jews and people of color were not equal to whites. Hitler hoped that these Olympics would prove he was right.

Jesse Owens was the star of the 1936 Olympic Games. He won the 100-meter dash. Ralph Metcalfe,

At the 1936 Olympics, some people did not believe that Jesse and the other black athletes were as good as the white athletes.

On the first day of the Olympics, Jesse beat all the other runners in the first trial run of the 100-meter race.

who was also an African American, came in second. Then, Jesse won the 200-meter dash. Matthew Robinson, another black man, came in second.

Other black athletes did very well too. Cornelius Johnson, David Albritton, and Delos Thurber won the gold, silver, and bronze medals in the high jump. Adolf Hitler was very upset.

Jesse broke the world record for the broad jump at the Olympics.

CHAPTER 4
A GOOD SPORT

Jesse was doing very well at the Olympics. Then something went wrong in the broad jump event. People were surprised that the great Jesse Owens was in trouble. When he did his first jump, he thought it was a practice jump. But it wasn't. Now he had only two more tries. If he missed these jumps, he would not make it into the final round.

Jesse got set. He did his next jump. "Scratched," the judge shouted. Jesse's foot was over the white line. The jump didn't count. He had only one more jump left. If he missed this jump, he was out.

Luz Long was a very good broad jumper. Luz was Germany's best hope for a gold medal in this event. He spoke to Jesse. His English was not very good. "I am Luz Long," he said. "You need to calm yourself." He smiled at Jesse. The two young men talked until

Jesse felt calmer. Jesse's last jump was good. He would compete against Luz in the **finals**.

Jesse beat Luz Long in the final broad jump and set a world record. Luz surprised everyone. He raised Jesse's arm and shouted, "Jesse . . . Jesse!" The crowd joined in and shouted "Jesse . . . Jesse!" People cheered for both Jesse and Luz. They were both winners.

Jesse was also part of the 400-meter relay team. He was not part of the original team. Jesse and his teammate Ralph Metcalfe replaced the two starting American runners, named Marty Glickman and Sam Stoller.

Some people believe that Glickman and Stoller were replaced because they were Jewish. They were very angry. But Glickman and Stoller still cheered when the American 400-meter relay team won first place. Jesse had won another gold medal. He went home with four gold medals.

Jesse never saw Luz Long again. Luz was killed in World War II. After the war ended, Jesse went back to Germany. He visited Luz's family. Jesse told them what Luz had done for him at the Olympics. The families became friends.

CHAPTER 5
REACH FOR GREATNESS

Jesse had married his high school sweetheart, Ruth Solomon, in 1935. They had three daughters: Gloria, Beverly, and Marlene.

Jesse faced some tough times after the Olympics. When he first came home, Jesse was treated like a star. People offered him many business deals. Jesse tried to be fair and honest. He believed other people were fair and honest, too. He was wrong. A lot of people were not fair with Jesse. He lost a lot of money.

Jesse started some businesses that worked out well. Others failed. Jesse went back to Ohio State for a while. He was not a very good student.

Jesse enjoyed working with children. He was very good at helping start youth athletic programs. He worked for the Recreation Department of Cook County (Chicago), Illinois. He told young children all over America to "reach for greatness."

Jesse Owens became famous for his great talent. He used his fame to help others, especially young people.

By the 1960s, African Americans had won some rights, but there was still **prejudice**. There were still many black people who were poor. They had little hope of doing better, and African Americans were angry.

Jesse wrote a book called *Blackthink* in 1970. He said that African Americans did not get ahead because they did not want to. Many people did not like the book. They wrote angry letters to Jesse. Some of the letters said that Jesse was too famous to know about prejudice against African Americans.

Jesse read these letters carefully. He thought again about the problems of African Americans. In 1972, he wrote another book, called *I Have Changed*. In this book, he apologized for some of the things he said in *Blackthink*.

Jesse was given many honors in his life. In February 1979, **President** Jimmy Carter gave Jesse an award at the White House. President Carter said, "He has always helped others to reach for greatness."

Jesse Owens died of lung cancer on March 31, 1980, in Tucson, Arizona. He was 66 years old.

WORDS TO KNOW

broad jump—A track and field event now called the long jump. Athletes compete to see how far they can jump. There are two events. In one, the athletes begin from a standing position. In the other, they get a running start.

dash—A short-distance running race.

finals—The championship competition in a sporting event.

Heil Hitler—This German phrase means *Hail Hitler*—or Praises to Hitler.

high jump—A track and field event. Athletes compete to see who can jump the highest. The athletes jump over a high bar and try not to knock it down.

Hitler, Adolf—The Nazi leader of Germany from 1933 to 1945.

Nazi—The political party in power in Germany from 1933 to 1945.

Olympics—A sporting event where athletes from all over the world compete for medals in all kinds of sports. The games are held every four years in different countries.

prejudice—A dislike of people, places, or things without a good reason.

president—The leader of a country or an organization.

track and field—A sport that includes running, jumping, and throwing.

world record—The best performance in the world of a sports event.

LEARN MORE

BOOKS

Braun, Eric. *Jesse Owens*. Mankato, Minn.: Capstone Press, 2005.

Oxlade, Chris. *Olympics*. New York: DK Publishing, 2005.

Weatherford, Carol Boston. *Jesse Owens: Fastest Man Alive*. New York: Walker & Co., 2006.

WEB SITES

The Jesse Owens Foundation
Learn about Jesse Owens's life as well as the many programs created thanks to his generosity.

<http://www.jesse-owens.org>

Jesse Owens: Olympic Legend
This site has a biography and photographs of Jesse Owens.

<http://www.jesseowens.com/about/.html>

INDEX